YOUR COMPANION AFTER SEXUAL ASSAULT

CHAPTERS BY GRETA SMITH
DEVOTIONS BY EMILY FLEMMING

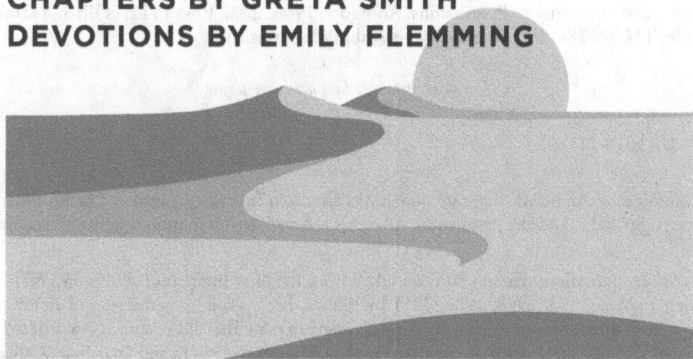

OUT OF
THE DEPTHS

Abingdon Press
Nashville

OUT OF THE DEPTHS:
YOUR COMPANION AFTER SEXUAL ASSAULT

Copyright © 2018 by Abingdon Press

This book is printed on acid-free paper.

978-1-5018-7138-2

18 19 20 21 22 23 24 25 26 27—10 9 8 7 6 5 4 3 2 1
MANUFACTURED IN THE UNITED STATES OF AMERICA

CONTENTS

CONTENTS

INTRODUCTION

For God alone my soul waits in silence;
*   from him comes my salvation.*
He alone is my rock and my salvation,
*   my fortress; I shall never be shaken.*

How long will you assail a person,
*   will you batter your victim, all of you,*
*   as you would a leaning wall, a tottering fence?...*

For God alone my soul waits in silence,
*   for my hope is from him.*
He alone is my rock and my salvation,
*   my fortress; I shall not be shaken.*
On God rests my deliverance and my honor;
*   my mighty rock, my refuge is in God....*

Once God has spoken;
*   twice have I heard this:*
that power belongs to God,
*   and steadfast love belongs to you, O Lord.*
For you repay to all
*   according to their work.*

—Psalm 62 (NRSV)

Mary[1] looked the part of the quintessential grandmother. Her face was etched with fine lines. Her gray hair was pulled up and neatly pinned back. Her wire rimmed glasses were balanced delicately on the bridge of her nose. When she smiled, her blue eyes sparkled. Today, though, her spirit was heavy. Her smiles were few and far between.

I was a graduate student in clinical psychology assigned to provide services under supervision at a local community mental health center, and Mary was one of my first clients. She had been referred by her primary care physician due to concerns about deepening depression. Mary was in her sixties, and although she had struggled with depression for years, she had never talked to a counselor before.

In the first session, Mary shared with me that she had felt depressed off and on for much of her adult life. She had subscribed to the mentality of powering through, pulling herself up by her bootstraps, and going on. Lately, however, for reasons she did not understand, this approach was not working. She was frequently tearful. She had been able to hide her sadness from her husband and family for years but now found herself no longer able to put on a happy face. She did not see how talking could help, but she was a good patient and followed her doctor's advice. Still skeptical after meeting once, she agreed to schedule a second appointment.

In the next appointment, Mary made a bold and courageous decision. She announced to me that she believed her depression might be related to something that troubled her from her past. She had a secret, one which she had never disclosed to anyone—not to family or friends, not even to her husband of forty years. After testing the waters gently, Mary tearfully confided that she had been repeatedly sexually assaulted as a child. She had been forbidden under threat of harm from sharing this secret, but she likely would have kept it anyway. It made her feel dirty and ashamed. Intuitively, she also felt that telling it would have emotionally shattered her mother.

I was young and inexperienced, but I knew that I had been entrusted with a precious confidence. I felt the enormous weight of it. Mary had trusted me, a relative stranger, with her wounded soul. My response was crucial. While this was an opportunity to help Mary find relief, I could, with the wrong words, easily add to her pain. I was overcome with empathy and with anxiety of my own.

I had no wisdom to offer Mary, but I could listen. So that is what I did. The theme that stood out the most to me as Mary shared her story was the easy way in which she accepted the blame for what had happened to her. Somehow, though she was now in her sixties, her mind reasoned about these events as if she were a school-aged girl. As she told me about them, she made everything out to be her own fault.

It just so happened that Mary had a granddaughter who was about the same age she had been during the abuse. I remember talking about what could be expected of a girl that age. How does she relate to the adults she trusts? How would she respond to the harmful actions and betrayal of those she depended upon to care for her? I encouraged Mary to spend some time with her granddaughter, to realize—to really notice—that she was a child, not an adult. I asked her if she could have the same compassion toward herself at that age as she would have toward her own grandchild. She was quiet, and I could not read her reaction. When Mary left the office that day, my heart was heavy. I felt as if I had done very little to help her.

In the next session, though, Mary presented in a different frame of mind. Her spirit seemed lighter. Her mood was improving. She had been sleeping better, and she was not tearful as she had been before. She announced that she did not think she needed counseling anymore. She had gotten a huge secret off her chest. She felt liberated.

To humor me, as much as anything, she agreed to one more session. Once again, she returned with a lighter countenance, an ease and a peace about her spirit. Although she had still not shared her secret with anyone else, she felt that she did not need to. Once disclosed, it seemed that the abuse of her childhood no longer held the same power over her. She was free. We said our goodbyes, and I never saw Mary again.

At the time, I viewed my sessions with Mary as a treatment failure because she did not return. It seemed impossible to me that she had resolved the issues related to her childhood sexual abuse so quickly. I understood her leaving, in language often used in my profession, as a "flight from therapy." Perhaps Mary had disclosed too much too early, and as a result, needed to flee.

Twenty years later, I have a different view. Perhaps Mary did leave counseling too early. Perhaps I should have cautioned her about the effects of such a huge disclosure so soon. Perhaps she did run away. Perhaps, though, Mary simply knew that she had gotten what her soul needed then. Maybe she was healed. Maybe she never sought counseling again, or maybe she, like many people, returned to counseling later, in the midst of another struggle with depression or to address other issues related to her abuse history. Maybe a successful entrance into and exit from therapy made it possible for her to seek help again later. Maybe even exercising this level of autonomy—whether and how much to share and how long she would stay—was part of her healing. Regardless, Mary stands out in my mind as a brave soul who introduced me to themes I would revisit with other survivors of sexual abuse and sexual assault, particularly themes of power, shame, and the power of shame.

Scripture does not shy away from such themes. The Bible is filled with stories addressing difficult issues, like shame and the abuse of power. It calls out the abuse of power and promises the restoration of honor. In fact, correcting the abuse of power lies at the heart of the biblical narrative of justice. In the Bible, we learn that God is not unaware of the suffering inflicted upon God's children when power is misused, whether individually or systemically, including in sexual exploitation. There are narratives in which rape leads to retaliatory war (Gen 34; 2 Sam 13), and in the law of the Old Testament, committing a rape is punishable by death (see Lev 22:25-27). I believe that the inclusion of these stories in the Bible demonstrates God's concern for those who have been violated and afflicted by the devastating effects of such abuse, and who are, sadly, numerous.

According to the National Sexual Violence Resource Center[2]:

- 1 in 4 girls and 1 in 6 boys will be sexually abused before the age of 18

- 1 in 5 women and 1 in 16 men are sexually assaulted while in college

- 1 in 5 women and 1 in 71 men will be raped at some point during their lives

- More than 1/3 of women who report being raped before the age of 18 also report being raped again as an adult

- In 8 out of 10 cases of rape, the victim knew the perpetrator

- Rape is the most under-reported crime

- Only 12% of child sexual abuse is reported to the authorities

These statistics clearly demonstrate the prevalence of sexual violence within our society. It is a crime of epic proportions. What the statistics fail to adequately show is the depth and breadth of the effects of such trauma. And certainly, they fail to adequately communicate the level of personal pain and suffering each number represents. They cannot tell the full story of the impact of every individual case of sexual trauma. Your particular story, whatever it entails, is a case in point. Words and numbers will never be adequate to describe your suffering. No one knows it fully, except you, and perhaps even you are struggling to understand all that it encompasses. There is One, though, who knows it all—every detail and every consequence. God sees your inmost broken places, and desires to heal them. Furthermore, and most importantly, God is completely capable of doing so. I fully believe that.

This little book is intended to support your healing from the experience of sexual trauma. It is organized into two parts. The first is educational. In it, we will look at five of the most helpful things to know about sexual assault and the healing process. It is my hope that this knowledge will provide a useful frame for your personal experience and will help you on your journey toward peace and wholeness. The second part of the book is devotional and consists of thirty scripture readings, devotions, and prayers written by my co-author from a supportive and restorative perspective. It is my prayer that these readings will be a balm for your soul, provide a daily grounding faith ritual, and be a source of connection to God and another during a time which can feel isolating, lonely and overwhelming. You do not have to read the first part of this book before beginning the devotions. Feel free to start them at any time.

The first part of this book draws from my experience of more than 15 years as a practicing mental health professional, from the many courageous souls who have taught me about healing from sexual assault, and from my expertise on trauma and recovering from it. While no two people will experience or be affected by sexual trauma exactly the same way—factors like personal and relational history, personality characteristics, and additional stressors and supports will determine how such trauma affects people differently—there tend to be common themes, and an introduction to these may be especially helpful in your healing process. As we examine them together, I will refer to the example of Mary. Although the details of your assault may be different from hers,

I pray that she may be a source of hope and inspiration to you as she has been to me. I have thought of her many times over the course of my career, with the prayer that she had indeed found the peace, comfort, and healing she so desired and deserved.

In my work as a counselor, I have been privileged to listen to the stories of countless individuals who have experienced horrific, even indescribable, trauma. I am continually awed by the grace of God and the resilience of the human spirit in the lives of those who survive and even thrive following such personal tragedy. No matter your experience, I am convinced that you can survive and thrive, too.

If this little book has found its way into your hands, please know that I am profoundly sorry for the harm that has been done to you. Remember that you are not alone. You are joined by many individuals across the ages who know the particular pain of sexual trauma. Remember, too, that you are loved and cherished by a God who resurrects the *body* as well as the soul. God cares about you in your entirety, and the integrity of your body is especially important to God. I have faith that God yearns to heal you, wholly and completely. I pray that you will feel the redeeming power of God's touch upon you, comforting you, strengthening you, and sustaining you in the days, weeks, and years ahead.

God, may my soul find rest in you. When I feel broken and betrayed, assaulted and ignored, be my refuge and fortress. Heal me, my body and my soul. Remove my shame in my own eyes, reminding me that I was never shamed in yours. Strip the power of those who have harmed me, that they would be able to hurt me no more. Instead, convince me that all power belongs to you, and that with you is unfailing love. In time, may I learn to trust again.
Amen.

Blessings and peace,
Greta Smith

Chapter One

PSYCHOLOGICAL AND PHYSIOLOGICAL EFFECTS OF SEXUAL ASSAULT

When we have experienced any kind of trauma, it is normal to feel disoriented, disrupted, and disorganized by the experience. Our brains are built to process information and to make sense of the world around us. When something happens to us that threatens our safety, when we feel helpless or defenseless, or when we are caught off guard, our brains often work overtime to try to process that experience so that we can protect ourselves better in the future. Sometimes this extra work is productive, and sometimes it is counterproductive. Regardless, we may find ourselves struggling with questions about what happened. Common questions sexual assault survivors struggle with include:

- Why did this happen to me? How did it happen? Did I somehow cause it?

- Is what I'm going through normal? Does anyone else feel this way?

- How long will I feel like this?

- Who can I trust? Will I ever feel safe again?

In wrestling with these questions, it is important to keep in mind that sexual assault is a trauma with both psychological and physical components and often has strong physical ramifications alongside the psychological ones. Re-establishing a sense of safety, security and trust are key factors in healing.

Simply put, traumatic events are those that cause bodily or psychological harm, pain, or fear, exceeding our capacity to cope. Trauma expert Bessel van der Kolk defines trauma as "an event that overwhelms the central nervous system...that you are incapable of assimilating, of taking in and integrating."[1] According to the American Psychological Association, almost half of people will be exposed to at least one traumatic event in their lifetime.[2] Most will adjust and adapt to the experience over time, returning to their previous level of functioning, but others will experience long-lasting effects such as depression and anxiety. About eight percent will develop post-traumatic stress disorder, which is characterized by re-experiencing of the event(s) through intrusive memories, nightmares, or flashbacks; avoidance behaviors such as altering activities to avoid reminders of the event; altered mood or cognitions such as inability to remember significant aspects of the trauma or feelings of detachment; and altered arousal or reactivity such as increased startle response, and/or dissociating (feeling a sense of not being within one's body or that things are not real) when confronted with reminders of the event(s).[3]

Researchers have learned some valuable insights in recent years about the way the brain is affected by trauma, and these insights have significant implications for healing and treatment. When we are threatened with harm, our brains shift into survival mode. In the interest of staying alive, the sensory information we take in is processed quickly in the most primitive part of our brains. Rather than act, we react. In other words, the part of our brains that is responsible for higher reasoning, planning, and organization tends to become suspended or disengaged. Instead of thoughtfully processing what is happening to us and systematically choosing a course of action, we are more likely to respond quickly and automatically or to shut down entirely. The part of our brains that takes over is called the limbic system, and it is the part where our emotions are seated. Its primary job is to keep us alive and safe.

The limbic system is not concerned with understanding what happened or with keeping us content and healthy. For the brain, if it comes down to feeling emotionally-grounded and well versus ensuring our continued safety, the limbic system will win every time with its fight, flight, or freeze response. Therein lies the problem for survivors of trauma. Sometimes following trauma, for lack of a better way to say it, the limbic system hijacks the rest of the brain. A person becomes stuck in a state of hyperawareness and hyperarousal. Sleeping is difficult. Eating is difficult. He or she is always on alert. Flashes of traumatic memories keep the person on edge, always ready to freeze, fight or flee. This is the kind of counterproductive "overtime" work of the brain that I referred to earlier.

Calming the hyper-alert limbic system and re-establishing a sense of safety is of the utmost importance following any traumatic event. Usually, it is helpful to reprocess the event by talking or writing about it or using other forms of self-expression. This engages the higher-order thinking parts of the brain, such as the prefrontal cortex, to make sense of the trauma and to assimilate and integrate it in a healthy way, so that it is not as frightening or overwhelming. Because social support can also be an important factor in healing, talking to a trusted confidant and telling the story of what happened can be especially effective. For people who do not like to talk or share their feelings verbally, journaling, drawing, sculpting, other forms of art, and music can provide a valuable and healing means of communication. This kind of "brain work" can be productive.

In addition, sexual assault is a kind of trauma in that it involves physical violation and harm that is especially threatening to a person's sense of self. Although sexual assault does not necessarily involve the kind of physical trauma that results in the need for life-sustaining emergency medical treatment, the physical nature of sexual assault adds another dimension to its psychological damage. For one thing, the physical sensations of the assault become part of the body's memory of the trauma. For another, sexual trauma strikes at the core of a person's identity and integrity.

People who have been sexually violated often feel wounded in the deepest part of themselves and report that something vital and irreplaceable has been taken from them. Sexual assault, then, frequently involves a sense of loss. When something valuable has been lost, it will be grieved. Therefore, the trauma of sexual assault regularly includes its own grief process.

Our sexual organs (any part of the body involved in a sexual response) are the most private parts of ourselves. The invasion or exploitation of these organs marries physical and psychological pain in a way that few experiences do. Even more complicated is the relationship between pleasure and pain in the sexual response. Because of our biology, our bodies sometimes respond to stimuli in ways our brains do not understand. Especially in childhood, without a frame of reference for the experience of mature, healthy sexual intimacy, the physical sensations can be especially confusing.

When a person does not feel safe in their own body, they cannot feel safe anywhere. This is a common consequence of sexual assault. As Dr. van der Kolk writes, "Traumatized people chronically feel unsafe inside their bodies. The past is alive in the form of gnawing interior discomfort. Their bodies are constantly bombarded with visceral warning signs.... They develop a fear of fear itself."[4]

The issue is compounded when the assault was prolonged or repeated (as in many instances of childhood sexual abuse). When abuse has been prolonged or involves repetitive encounters, there is not a singular memory of it but an amalgam of them. Healing may be more complicated. There is also a greater risk of posttraumatic stress when trauma is especially intense or long-lasting or when it occurs in childhood and involves a developing brain. In fact, much ongoing research seeks to identify how trauma affects brain development in childhood. In 1998, a landmark study found a link between a history of childhood abuse and many of the leading causes of death in adults.[5] This study was not limited to childhood sexual abuse, but it and subsequent research on Adverse Childhood Experiences (ACEs) have continued to uncover the added vulnerabilities of trauma in childhood. You can find more information about ACEs on the CDC website.[6]

In Mary's case, the sexual assault she experienced was both prolonged and repeated. It was in all likelihood causally related to the depressive episodes she had experienced off and on throughout her adult life. Given the extent and nature of the abuse Mary suffered, we now know that she was at greater risk for a variety of physical illnesses and emotional issues than her peers who were not abused. But research also helps shed light on another facet of Mary's story—her resilience. That Mary had not reached out for help before her sixties may have been a result of some of the protective factors within her environment.

For example, growing up, Mary had a close relationship with a supportive adult. Her relationship with her mother was strong. Although she had not reported the abuse to her mother, she made this decision out of love as much as fear. As counterintuitive as it sounds, in this way,

Mary preserved her relationship with her mother and it continued to serve as a haven for her. It is likely that Mary's mother's death served as the event that finally precipitated the depression that brought her into her doctor's office for treatment.

In addition, in adulthood, Mary had a strong marriage. Her husband was a friend and partner whose support, though he was also oblivious to the secret of her past, helped mitigate the lasting effects of her childhood trauma such that they were, for the most part, bearable.

In order to determine what you need most to heal from your assault, first take some time to notice what you are experiencing and how you are being affected. It seems obvious, but often when we are traumatized, we lose a sense of self-awareness. Your symptoms may be physiological, involving altered sleep and appetite, headaches or other aches or pains, or being easily startled. They may be emotional, including fear and anxiety, anger, irritability, tearfulness and sadness, mood swings, feelings of shame, guilt and self-blame, a sense of "numbness," or even a sense of unreality. They may be cognitive, characterized by confusion and difficulty concentrating, flashbacks or intrusive memories, wondering whether you are damaged, bad, or dirty, thinking "what if" or "if only," or questioning, "why me?" They may be social, such as social withdrawal, feeling distant and uncomfortable around people, fear of being alone, nervousness in crowds, a loss of trust, and difficulties with intimacy, especially sexual intimacy. Or they may involve all the above.

Healthy sexual intimacy is reciprocal, generous, and creative. By contrast, sexual assault is exploitative, self-centered and destructive. As you recover from its effects, in particular, you may need time to restore a sense of trust, tenderness, and enjoyment to sexual intimacy. You may need to consciously differentiate healthy sexuality from the trauma of assault, keeping in mind these characteristics. And you may need to ask your partner for help and patience in doing so.

Although symptoms can continue for weeks to months or arise weeks to months after the trauma, they are likely to dissipate over time. The question of whether to seek help in the form of counseling or psychotherapy is best answered by thinking about the extent of symptoms and the amount of time that has elapsed. More about this can be found in the final section of this essay. In general, though, if months have passed and your symptoms are not improving or are worsening, reach out for help. Moreover, if your symptoms are significantly interfering with your ability to function day-to-day, seek help no matter how long it has been since the assault.

Trauma affects people differently, and while there is no "one size fits all" approach to healing from trauma generally or from sexual assault specifically, there are some things that seem to be helpful for most people. As I mentioned before, communicating in some way about the assault, whether by talking with a trusted friend, a therapist, or a support group or through journaling, music or art, can help the brain process the memories and emotions associated with it. However, talking or communicating about the experience may not be enough. More and more, researchers who study trauma and therapists who work with trauma survivors are noting the connection between the body and the mind, and the significance of a "whole person" approach to healing. Engaging the body to heal both the body and the mind has gathered increasing interest and support within the therapeutic community. To quote Bessel van der Kolk again, "Talking, understanding and human connections help, and drugs can dampen hyperactive alarm systems. But we will also see that the imprints from the past can be transformed by having physical experiences that directly contradict the helplessness, rage, and collapse that are part of trauma, and thereby regaining self-mastery."[7]

What this means for you is that practices that highlight the connection between the body and the mind could be integral to regaining a healthy body awareness and physical sense of calm and safety. Yoga is wonderful for this and has been beneficial for many people, but other forms of physical activity that engage the attention mindfully could have the same effect. Walking, hiking, or running with awareness of your movement and the breath and attention to the senses in the present moment—what you see, hear, feel, smell, taste—might feel more suited to your particular personality and needs. Massage and other touch therapies by a trusted, qualified professional can also be helpful. Find what works for you, but do not neglect the importance of your body in the healing process. Trauma, we now know, becomes lodged in the body as well as the mind. To re-establish safety, security, and trust, you must make friends again with your body as well as your mind. Body awareness and physical experiences that help you regain a sense of bodily integrity, mastery, and pleasure will be an essential part of your recovery.

Chapter Two

RECLAIMING YOUR POWER

In the 1970's a feminist theorist brought much-needed attention to the problem of rape by declaring it to be about power and not about sex.[1] This thinking was revolutionary at the time and helped shift the focus of our understanding of rape from the victims to the perpetrators. The societal tendency to blame the victim in cases of sexual assault rather than look at the cultural determinants and psychological factors that supported what we now call "rape culture" led to Brownmiller's groundbreaking assertion. Today we know that to say sexual assault is only about power oversimplifies the complex personal, social, and biological factors involved in sexual assault. We also know that it does not make sense to declare that a sexual act is not at all about sex. The truth is that most behaviors, including sexual assault, are multidetermined. However, I still think it is safe to say that sexual assault is an act of aggression *as much as* it is a sexual act. It is a form of violence that is sexual in nature.

There are still strong social forces in place which tend to ignore or downplay cases of sexual assault or to blame the victim. Sexual objectification is still much more socially acceptable in our culture than violence. Realizing that you have been the victim of a violent act has important consequences for how you understand that act and for how you heal and move forward. But let's start with an understanding of sexual assault as an act of interpersonal violence, motivated for the perpetrator by either a sense of power or a sense of powerlessness.

Cultures in which there are higher rates of interpersonal violence, in which women are excluded from positions of power and are objectified, and those in which there are rigid sex-role divisions, tend to have higher rates of sexual violence.[2] Likewise, if we try to understand sexual assault from an individual psychological perspective, we can identify risk factors for the commission of assault from the research literature, including low self-esteem and low empathy, deviant sexual arousal, poor mental health, a tendency toward cognitive distortion (important for rationalizing the behavior), a history of childhood abuse and parental violence, attachment disorders, alcohol and drug abuse, and juvenile delinquency, among others.[3] These findings remind us that cultural brokenness and individual pathology are the most significant underlying causes of sexual assault.

While it is normal after experiencing a trauma to revisit the circumstances surrounding it, to look for some way we might have prevented it from happening, or to wonder if we somehow caused it, examining the social and cultural factors that contribute to sexual assault can be empowering for you as a survivor. In addition, be aware that psychological, environmental, developmental, situational, and biological factors were all involved in determining the behavior of the perpetrator of the violence against you. These, and not who you are, how you look, or what you did, were the primary determinates. You did not bring this upon yourself. In all likelihood, if you had not been the victim, someone else would have been. Perhaps you are even aware of others who were victimized by the same perpetrator. While I realize that this knowledge provides little or no comfort for the distress you have endured, it may help you release yourself from misplaced and unhealthy guilt or self-blame.

Remember the example of Mary? In her case the power dynamics are clear. She was a minor, and the perpetrator of her sexual trauma was an adult who had authority over her. She was in a position of dependence and powerlessness. You would not hesitate to call what happened to her oppressive and unjust. Perhaps in the case of your assault the power dynamics were not as clear prior to the assault. Regardless, the person who violated you assumed control over something that did not belong to them—your body. This act was an abuse of power, and it, too, was oppressive and unjust. Dominating and assuming power over another is an aggressive act. It can be accomplished by physical overpowering, intimidation, or fear. If you did not consent to the sexual act, it was an act of aggression, and *it was wrong, period.*

Identifying power and aggression dynamics in sexual assault has implications for healing from it. Empowerment is an important part of healing for many survivors. When a person feels like their sense of mastery and agency has been taken away, regaining it is important. There are multiple transformative ways to approach empowerment. To begin with, taking control of one's own health and healing by actively seeking out education, counseling, and support can be empowering. Even picking up this little book and reading it is a step toward empowerment! Others find a sense of empowerment by taking a personal safety or self-defense class. Many local law enforcement agencies offer personal safety classes, as do some martial arts centers.

If your sexual assault has resulted in criminal charges, then involvement in the prosecution and conviction of the perpetrator can also be empowering. However, a few words of caution are very important here. First of all, be careful not to take on a sense of responsibility for the outcome of any investigation or trial involving the perpetrator. Our justice system is flawed and in need of repair, and while survivors are often empowered by seeing justice served, they are also often, sadly, re-traumatized by seeing justice fail.

Because of the traumatic nature of sexual assault, the re-traumatization often involved in reporting it, and the uncertainty surrounding the outcome, it is not surprising that 2 out of 3 sexual assaults go unreported.[4] I have always counseled survivors that whether to report is a decision only they can make and that it is okay to choose self-preservation over justice and social change, with one exception. When there has been childhood sexual abuse and the victim is still underage and/or the perpetrator could be in the position of abusing other children, a report should be made to Child Protective Services in your state. Not only is this the right thing to do, it is mandatory by law in many states.

Following time to heal, social activism provides yet another avenue of empowerment for some. However, remember to treat yourself gingerly and not try to take on the world before or unless you are ready. Social activism can also be emotionally draining, and for those not properly trained, equipped, and supported, it can have the opposite rather than the intended effect, creating a sense of futility rather than empowerment. Creating cultural awareness and change is a long process that requires patience and perseverance. Be careful and attend to your emotional and spiritual needs first. Those who have invested in the development of inner strength and wellness are the ones best equipped to change the world.

At the time I am writing this, we are in the midst of what I and many hope will be a social revolution. The #MeToo and #TimesUp movements have helped uncover an ongoing culture of sexual harass-ment and assault and opened a much-needed social dialogue around change and transformation. I hope that this increased attention to an enduring social problem helps you realize both that you are not alone and that you are not to blame for the trauma you have sustained. I hope it encourages us all to participate in promoting a culture of change.

Chapter Three

DISARMING SHAME

Many sexual assault survivors experience shame related to the trauma they endured. Shame is a powerful emotion, and one which can have significant adverse effects on healing from trauma. Shame is the painful experience of humiliation, a loss of a sense of integrity, value and self-worth. It is normal to feel ashamed when the integrity of one's body has been violated. Popular writer and shame researcher Brené Brown writes that shame is "the intensely painful feeling or experience of believing that we are flawed and therefore unworthy of love and belonging."[1] I think her definition captures the two most significant aspects of the experience of shame. Shame makes us feel less than others, and, consequently, shame isolates us from others. When we are ashamed, we feel defective. As a result, we want to hide.

I could not find good research numbers on the prevalence of shame among survivors of sexual assault, but clinical experience suggests to me that it is high. What research does suggest is that continued feelings of shame can keep survivors from healing and moving forward to find meaning and joy in life again. Persistent shame has been linked to posttraumatic stress disorder in survivors of childhood sexual abuse, and research has suggested that it is important to cognitively and emotionally confront shame (in addition to fear) in processing traumatic experiences.[2]

Shame is part of the experience of sexual trauma in part because sexuality and sexual activity themselves are often a source of social disgrace. One of the most common reasons given by victims for not reporting sexual assault is not wanting anyone to know.[3] This is partly due to the social embarrassment around sexuality and partly to the continued culture of self-blame and self-consciousness surrounding sexual assault discussed earlier. In cases of childhood sexual abuse, which has been enveloped in secrecy and which may have been accompanied by verbal condemnation of the victim or by threats of harm if the secret is revealed, shame is prevalent.

Feelings of shame, while often part of the experience of sexual trauma, must be differentiated from self-blame. You may feel ashamed of what happened to you, but that does not mean you are shameful. You may *feel* flawed or unworthy, but that does not make it so. The shame you feel is a result of what happened to you. It did not cause what happened to you. This is an important distinction. When we feel unworthy, our minds tend to follow those feelings of unworthiness down the rabbit hole. We draw mistaken conclusions, and can too easily concoct a story that we somehow deserved the bad things that have happened to us.

The question, then, for survivors of sexual assault, is what disarms shame? How do those who heal from sexual trauma successfully navigate the waters of shame and move on? According to Dr. Brown, whose work on shame and vulnerability has sparked a cultural conversation around these topics, shame thrives in secrecy, silence, and judgment. The antidote to shame, then, is to share the secret and break the silence in a safe and trustworthy environment. While shame thrives on judgment and criticism, it is broken by empathy and acceptance.[4]

Remember how Mary so easily, even though she was a child, made herself out to be responsible for the abuse she experienced? In retrospect, I understand the disarming of shame to be the greatest contributor to her positive response in counseling. Mary had been ashamed to tell the story of her abuse. For all of her life, she had struggled under the weight of the secret and the fear of what might happen if she disclosed it. Who would be hurt? What would other people think? Would she be told that the abuse was her fault, as she deeply feared? Mary expected to be criticized and blamed. When her disclosure was met instead with understanding, acceptance, and empathy, her shame dissipated. She was able to receive compassion and support, and then she was able to offer it to herself just as she would to someone she loved dearly, like her granddaughter. This was transformative for Mary.

If you are struggling with feelings of shame, confiding in even one other person about the trauma you have experienced could be a giant leap forward in your healing. You do not have to share your story openly with everyone or even with multiple people in order to experience relief from shame, and you do not have to share all of the details of it.

However, you do need to choose someone who is trustworthy and who can be expected to respond with empathy and understanding. If there is no one in your circle—a family member, friend, or pastor, for example—in whom you can confide or if you are too uncertain of the response to risk it, seek out a counselor or support group. And if for some unforeseen reason you do confide in someone who shames you further, please know that it is imperative that you not give up and stop there. In such a circumstance, unchecked shame is likely to grow exponentially and may make you more vulnerable to additional emotional pain and turmoil. Find someone else who will listen nonjudgmentally, with tenderness and empathy.

Most of all, remember the compassion of your Creator. I began this essay with an appeal made by the psalmist to find rest in God. The psalmist seeks refuge from assailants and restoration of honor (verses 3-8), with a proclamation of and appeal to the power of God (verse 11). The psalmist remembers God's unfailing love (verse 12).

I chose Psalm 62 because the language of this song encompasses the main themes I wanted to address, but the Psalms and many other passages of scripture are rich with descriptions of the compassion, tenderness, lovingkindness, and healing presence of God. Prayer is an important means for us, as people of faith, to experience God's compassion and redemption. Confide in God as you would a friend, and even if you do not feel unburdened right away, continue the practice. Make certain that you take the time to listen, also. I am confident that you will feel God's broken-heartedness over your suffering and experience God's lovingkindness and tender care, binding your wounds.

There is one more consideration for our discussion of the experience of shame. Be aware that shame may not completely resolve and may from time to time rear its ugly head. It is important to know the kinds of things that trigger feelings of shame for you (as well as other feelings and thoughts related to the assault) so that you are not caught off guard and derailed by them. Identifying triggers helps you more quickly recover from shame when it arises because you can then both name the feeling and put it in its proper place. Triggers, over time, will lose their ability to incapacitate you by stealing your sense of self or self worth.

Chapter Four

PRACTICING SELF-COMPASSION

ompassion should be a familiar practice for followers of Jesus Christ, whose divine nature is that of love and forgiveness, and whose humanity and earthy ministry were characterized by compassion as much as anything. As Christians, we are taught to show mercy and compassion and to believe that by God's grace, God is ever transforming our hearts to become more compassionate. Most of us, however, are much better at practicing compassion toward others than showing compassion for ourselves.

Several years ago, a psychologist by the name of Kristin Neff decided to define and study the concept of self-compassion. She has since linked self-compassion to psychological well-being and increased resilience from psychological distress.[1] Self-compassion, simply put, is having compassion for oneself in the same way that one has compassion for another. Dr. Neff has found that there are three components of self-compassion: self-kindness rather than self-judgement, common humanity rather than isolation, and mindfulness rather than over-identification.

Self-kindness rather than self-judgement refers to the inner dialogue that takes place about the events of our lives that precipitate stress and suffering. When we are operating out of self-judgment, we engage in the kind of self-blame discussed earlier. At best, we berate ourselves for our behavior—our mistakes, our failures, our bad decisions and poor choices. At worst, we berate ourselves not only for our behavior and choices but for our very being. We say things to ourselves like, "I am stupid;" "I am unworthy;" or even "I am nothing." You can see the relationship of self-judgment to shame. Such negative self-talk is akin to shaming ourselves. It goes hand in hand with the feeling of being unworthy of love and belonging.

By contrast, self-kindness involves a different kind of self-talk, one that is forgiving of mistakes, failures, and shortcomings. Instead of saying, "I am a mistake," self-kindness might say, "I made a mistake. Everyone makes mistakes." Instead of saying, "I am suffering because I deserve it. I am unworthy," self-kindness might say, "I am suffering because the world is imperfect, and everyone suffers." Self-compassionate people tend to be gentle with themselves in the face of trials and suffering. Self-compassionate people of faith see themselves as children of God, beloved and adored by God, and can treat themselves with the kindness God intends for them and for all of God's children.

Common humanity rather than isolation is a closely related concept. When self-compassionate people experience distress, they tend to use their experience of pain to identify with others rather than to distance themselves from others. While people who have less self-compassion tend to see themselves as suffering in isolation, thinking things like, "I am the only one who has experienced this kind of pain," self-compassionate people see suffering as part of the human condition. They have a sense that the experience of pain and uncertainty is common to all humanity.

Mindfulness rather than over-identification refers to the meta-awareness of emotional experience. Meta-awareness is awareness that "goes beyond." It is being aware of being aware. In other words, meta-awareness seeks not only to recognize emotional experience but to go above or beyond it. People who cultivate mindfulness are developing meta-awareness of their emotional experience and neither ignore it nor are swept away by it. They can observe their thoughts and feelings without judgement or fear, and without "over-identifying" with them, cognizant that thoughts and emotions change over time. It is a balanced approach to emotional experience. By contrast, over-identification occurs when we are swept away by our thoughts and feelings. We become reactive and overly influenced by negative thoughts and feelings.

Cultivating self-compassion, then, involves treating ourselves with kindness, recognizing our common humanity, and practicing mindfulness. We treat ourselves with kindness and recognize our common humanity when we consciously change a negative inner dialogue. We stop ourselves when we realize that we are being self-critical and isolating, and we purposefully change our self-talk by introducing self-acceptance and forgiveness and recognizing the universality of our experience. We instead say the kinds of things to ourselves that we would say to a friend who is struggling with the same negative emotions. We practice mindfulness by cultivating self-awareness. We turn our attention to the present moment, paying attention to our thoughts and feelings and noticing how they change over time. Practicing self-compassion takes time. It is not something that can be learned in a day. Continue to nurture it, however, and you will see it develop over time.

I believe self-compassion was instrumental in Mary's experience of freedom from the trauma of her childhood sexual abuse. By observing her granddaughter and imagining herself at the age during which the abuse occurred, she was able to exercise the same compassion toward herself that she would toward a child. Rather than continuing to criticize and blame herself for the abuse, she began to feel sad for and protective of the little girl who had been exploited. In addition, Mary was able to realize that she was not alone in her experience of being exploited and abused. In sharing her story, she learned that childhood sexual abuse was more prevalent than she thought. Because it was rarely talked about when Mary was a child and was only gaining increased attention and recognition when she made her disclosure, Mary had viewed the trauma as something that set her apart and made her different from everyone else. Feeling a sense of connection to others who had also suffered abuse further fostered her resilience.

Like self-compassion, forgiveness can be a powerful spiritual practice in the process of healing. Self-compassion is, I think, necessary first. Forgiveness is not something that should be forced out of guilt or because of the expectations of others. It cannot be forced before you are ready, but at the right time it can be empowering, freeing, and a key part of moving forward. Forgiveness, like self-compassion, is a process.

Some clarification is called for here about what forgiveness is and what it is not. Everett Worthington, a psychologist who has devoted his career to the study of forgiveness both in secular and Christian contexts, notes that there are two types of forgiveness, or perhaps two parts to it: decisional forgiveness and emotional forgiveness.[2] Decisional forgiveness involves making a decision to forgive and, for example, not seek revenge. It is possible, though, to make a decision to forgive and still harbor anger, resentment, fear, or other negative emotions toward the perpetrator. Emotional forgiveness, by contrast, involves releasing those negative emotions. When forgiving a stranger or someone with whom there is not a continued relationship, emotional forgiveness may simply mean returning to a state of having no emotion toward that person. In cases where the relationship continues, emotional forgiveness means replacing those negative feelings with positive ones such as compassion or empathy.

Forgiveness, however, does not imply that the harm that was done is acceptable. In addition, it is possible to decide to forgive someone and even to release negative emotion toward them and replace it with compassion and empathy but also to choose not to continue a relationship with them. Forgiveness of someone known to you who has hurt you does not necessarily imply reconciling and staying in relationship with them. Finally, deciding to practice forgiveness is not in conflict with deciding to pursue justice. It is possible to forgive and to seek justice at the same time. These are two distinct processes.

Dr. Worthington also reminds us that forgiveness is not an instantaneous process. A person may make an instantaneous decision to forgive, but emotions typically change over time, and not in a linear fashion. So, if you are working through forgiveness, you may think at times that you have released feelings of anger, hurt, or fear, only to find that they resurge. This is normal. Be patient, and, yes, *compassionate*, with yourself through the process.

Many people, once they have experienced decisional and emotional forgiveness, report it to be a liberating and empowering change. They often describe the sense that when they still held negative feelings toward the person who harmed them that person continued to dictate their lives to some degree. It was as if that person still had some power over them. They describe forgiveness as deeply freeing. The research of Dr. Worthington and others corroborates this experience, suggesting that forgiveness has physical, emotional, and relational benefits.[3]

I would like to offer one more observation about forgiveness. We know that an expression of remorse from the perpetrator helps victims and survivors forgive and move forward. However, in my clinical experience, expressions of remorse are the exception rather than the rule in cases of sexual abuse and sexual assault. It is important to realize this in order to have realistic expectations about your ability to forgive. It is possible (if not likely) that if you are to forgive, it will be without the benefit of an apology or other expression of guilt or remorse from the one or ones who hurt you. Know that you are not alone in this respect. Also know that a failure to express remorse means neither that there is none, nor that there was not cause for it. Whether remorse is acknowledged or not, what happened to you was unequivocally wrong. In addition, some perpetrators know that what they did was wrong and even know on some level to be sorry for it but are unable to express their remorse out of their own fragility and brokenness. This may be especially true for those perpetrators who were themselves once victims of abuse.

Chapter Five

RESOURCES FOR CONTINUED HEALING

Some people can heal from the trauma of sexual assault without seeking professional help. The redevelopment of a sense of safety and the ability to trust takes time, and you must be patient and gentle with yourself. However, research suggests that psychotherapy is effective and that qualified and experienced counselors can help facilitate recovery.[1] It is never too soon nor too late to seek help. Services for survivors of sexual assault are available in most communities and are often offered free of charge at clinics that specialize in sexual trauma. RAINN (Rape, Abuse and Incest National Network) is the nation's largest organization working to address sexual violence. Their website, www.rainn.org, has various resources, from information about how to seek needed medical care after an assault to navigating the criminal justice system to crisis and therapy services by location. They operate a national crisis hotline (800-656-HOPE) which can connect you with resources in your area. A search tool for local services can also be found on their website at www.centers.rainn.org.[2]

As I mentioned before, trauma survivors are at increased risk for anxiety and depression. About eight percent will develop post-traumatic stress disorder. If you experienced depression, anxiety, or another mental health condition prior to your assault, you are at increased risk for exacerbation of those conditions and/or development of additional symptoms. A history of other traumatic experiences also places you at increased risk, especially for post-traumatic stress disorder. Additional stressors, such as medical problems, relationship conflict, financial hardship, social or occupational stress, or a lack of social support can make you more vulnerable as well. If any of these circumstances applies to you, be aware of your increased vulnerability and do not hesitate to reach out for additional help and support as needed.

There are also some warning signs that warrant a conversation with your doctor or another medical or mental health professional right away. These include:

- Inability to sleep or eat

- Eating disorder symptoms, especially restricting calories or self-purging

- Extreme disruptions in ability to function, such as lack of self-care or care of dependent children

- Serious disruptions at work or in relationships

- Continued nightmares or re-experiencing of the trauma through flashbacks (these may be normal in the weeks immediately following the trauma)

- "Lost time," such as inability to remember hours or days, or being told of significant behaviors you do not remember

- Abuse of alcohol or drugs

- Any thoughts of self- or other- harm, including suicidal and homicidal thoughts and/or self-injury such as cutting

Any of these symptoms should be promptly evaluated by a medical or mental health provider.

Learn one final lesson from Mary. While our society prizes independence and self-reliance, we were not made to navigate the troubles of this world alone. Mary spent years shouldering a heavy burden and soldiering on. When she finally sought help and support, just a few sessions of talking seemed to give her immediate and substantial relief. Although most people do not experience the kind of relief Mary seemed to find so quickly, do not underestimate the difference a supportive ear can make in your healing. If Mary had reached out sooner, she might have saved herself significant distress and almost certainly would have saved herself from the deep loneliness she endured. Let her story be an inspiration to you. Help is available. It can be transformative.

The psalmist assures us that "the LORD is a safe place for the oppressed—a safe place in difficult times" (Ps 9:9). Sometimes the thing we need most is a safe place. The world does not always provide it. All of us are confronted at times with this realization. Fear can be a friend, helping us learn to protect and defend ourselves when needed; or it can become an enemy, keeping us from living the full and abundant lives we are meant to live. As you continue this journey of healing, pay attention to when fear is serving as the former for you and when it is serving as the latter.

Two of the primary motivating emotions in human behavior are fear and love. When people are motivated primarily by love, they move in the world to form relationships, to connect with others and give the best of themselves for the betterment of humanity. They can engage meaningfully to make the world a better place. When people are motivated primarily by fear, they tend to disconnect from the world and from others. They turn inward, and most of their energy necessarily goes toward self-protection, self-preservation, and recovery.

Following any traumatic event, it is both normal and necessary to turn inward and to focus on being safe and becoming well. Healing, whether physical or emotional, takes a tremendous amount of energy, and healing that is both physical *and* emotional takes extra work. Over time and with healing, though, love will begin to overcome fear as the driving force in your life once again. Keep this purpose in mind and believe that it is possible. Know that it was the way you were created and intended to live.

I began this essay by telling you about Mary, who found a safe place not so much inside of the counseling office as within herself. This is the ultimate therapeutic goal: to reclaim your body, mind, and spirit as a place of safety and serenity so that you may once again move forward in the world with love and purpose. I pray that the presence and the power of the Holy Spirit will surround you and work within you to transform your suffering, so that you, too, may find a safe place within yourself and carry it with you wherever you go.

#METOO

In 2017, celebrities, and then many other women and men, began posting on their social media accounts: "If all those who have been sexually harassed or assaulted will post #metoo, then we might get an idea of how widespread the problems are."

The avalanche began: first just a few, then thousands more. Some shared their stories, others just the hashtag. My friends wrote, "Hasn't every woman?" or "What's the point?" Others reminded us that not everyone feels safe enough to share. It was difficult to look at social media. As #metoo gained steam, more stories of victimization and violence popped up every day.

We cannot turn a blind eye to injustice and pain—our own or anyone else's. Jesus Christ calls us to compassion (from the Latin *com passio*, which means "with suffering"). We are called to be present to all forms of suffering, including our own. We cannot rush through the mess; we have to sit with it, not run away or bury our heads in the sand, pretending it never happened. Showing compassion to others is sometimes easier than being compassionate with ourselves, present to our own pain.

In the middle of this media storm, I felt a flash of comfort and solidarity when I saw a post echoing Matthew 25:40 (NRSV). Jesus speaks: "*Truly I tell you, just as you did it to one of the least of these who are members of my family, you did it to . . .*" #metoo.

It reminded me that even when I feel desperately alone and broken, Jesus Christ is with me for every painful, beautiful moment. He, too, was a survivor. I am never alone.

Remind me, God, that you are with me, even in the depths of this pain. Show me how to survive, how to be gentle with myself, and how to find my way back to you.

MAKE TIME FOR HEALING

Then the Spirit led Jesus up into the wilderness....
—Matthew 4:1a

By picking up this book, you have begun a journey of healing. But just like starting off on any journey (whether a road trip or a new relationship, job, or habit), it's best to blanket our start in prayer. When he began his formal ministry, Jesus went alone to the desert to get away from others, find silence, and seek a deep connection with God. He prepared for the difficult tasks ahead by grounding himself in God's love and presence.

When the Bible uses the phrase "forty days," it generally means any long period, anything outside of the normal way of marking time. To prepare ourselves for whatever lies ahead, we need to leave behind our schedules, plans, and the tiny spaces we've carved out for God and make room to truly experience wholeness and holiness.

During his forty days, Jesus choose not to eat. With each rumble of his stomach, he became more aware of God's presence. I am not encouraging fasting unless that is healthy for and helpful to you. But I do think we must take time out from our daily routines to focus on God if we want deep healing.

Jesus set aside both time and place. The wilderness was a symbol for any place outside of organized society. Monks and nuns for centuries have left normal life behind to live simply together and encounter God. Sometimes we, too, must pull ourselves out of our comfort zones and busy lives, which keep us frantic with activity. While we can't always fully escape our everyday life, we need a safe, quiet place, our own wilderness, where our deepest questions can surface. In the silence, we can listen for God's answers.

In my busy life, Lord, break into my routines of brokenness and send your healing power to stop me in my tracks and overwhelm me with your love!

SHOCK

No temptation has seized you that isn't common for people. But God is faithful. He won't allow you to be tempted beyond your abilities. Instead, with the temptation, God will also supply a way out so that you will be able to endure it.

—1 Corinthians 10:13

After an assault, life may feel impossible. I often woke up with no idea what to do next. The thought of taking a shower overwhelmed me. It required monumental energy to get dressed or leave the house. When I did, the whole world seemed different. The sun was too bright, and I felt like strangers were staring at me. I glanced quickly around, looking for danger even in "safe" places. I wondered if the people I passed knew what happened to me. I was shocked and annoyed at how carefree and happy everyone else seemed to be. I wanted to scream, "Don't you know that evil lurks in the shadows?" I could not focus or concentrate for weeks. I missed deadlines, forgot appointments, and skipped parties with friends. How could I live like this?

As I sat exhausted on a park bench one afternoon, 1 Corinthians 10:13 flashed into my ears, as if someone had audibly spoken it to me. I had memorized it as a teen at church camp, but I needed it in this moment.

I laughed loudly— I believed God had overestimated my strength! But that laughter broke through my zombie-like state, and I began to think about all the pain I had survived in my life before the assault. It was never on my own, but always through God's strength. Why was I trying to go it alone this time? Tears broke through as I prayed for the first time since my attack.

God, I miss laughter and feeling you with me. Where did you go? Where did I go? Bring me back, Lord, and remind me that my life and your love are my way out.

LOSING HOPE

The people walking in darkness have seen a great light.
On those living in a pitch-dark land, light has dawned.

—Isaiah 9:2

Soon after my assault, I wrote, "I sit in the complete darkness and pain of now, unable to remember joy from before, unable to conceive that hope will ever break through again. The weight of now threatens to extinguish me entirely." The feeling was real, even if I could not share it with others or if they chose not to believe me. Sometimes I could not see any path forward. I read books about trauma and healing, but I couldn't move the words through my brain and down into my heart. I was in a fog, like walking through a smoggy city. I was choking on the very air I breathed.

Before the assault, I believed that God was within me. During, I felt utterly alone. But afterward, I was just trying to pull myself back together from the broken shards left from the attack. Waiting for the light promised in Isaiah, I desperately wanted "now" to be over. I watched time slip by, but there was no end to the darkness. Then I read Leonard Cohen's words: "There is a crack in everything. That's how the light gets in."[1] That's also how the light gets out.

I realized that I wouldn't find hope or a path outside of me. The world kept spinning even though I had stepped off. But I didn't have to be ok or strong or to pull myself together. All I had to do was accept the pitch-dark around me and allow my cracks—this pain—to reveal the light from within me. The light of God's love and presence had always been there. I had simply forgotten it.

><><><><><><><><><><><><><><><><><><><><><

God of shards and smog, help me breathe again, to find a light and strength within me through you. I cannot do this alone!

><><><><><><><><><><><><><><><><><><><><><

1. Leonard Cohen, "Anthem." (Sony/ATV Music Publishing LLC, 1992.)

FEAR

Meanwhile, the boat, fighting a strong headwind, was being battered by the waves and was already far away from land.

—Matthew 14:24

To have fear is completely normal. Fear can help us to identify threats in violent situations. But when we focus solely on our fears, we cannot see God's hand leading us through storms. Take the example of Peter in Matthew 14:22-33. As the disciples sail across the Sea of Galilee, their boat is barely making it through the storm. There have been times when I've felt beaten up by life, far from the protection of God. That's when I am most afraid. When we are battered by the storms, if we look up, we may see Jesus walking toward us. I have never walked on water like Peter, but I have certainly gotten out of the boat and walked toward Jesus.

Soon, though, Peter felt a splash on his feet and immediately forgot who he was with. He began to think about where he was and what he was doing. Jesus had enabled him to walk on water; Jesus was literally standing right in front of him, but tiny doubts took hold and grew quickly into fear. Peter looked away for one moment and began to sink.

It is just that way with us. When we are focused on God, the impossible becomes possible. Jesus can conquer our storms, fears, and all dangers. When we take our eyes off him, though, we sink back into the depths of reality in our lives. Jesus never said that we would not face storms of difficulty and doubt, but he promised that if we focus on and trust in him, he will make us bold and strong. He gives us courage and protection. We are called to balance staring at and listening to our pain and fear with gazing into the face of our Creator, trusting that the Lord will protect us and restore our faith.

<><><><><><><><><><><><><><><><><><><><><><><><>

Holy One, thank you for always answering us immediately when we call out to you. Let us leave all of our hurts, doubts, and fears in your hands. Being lighter, let us start fresh in finding more joy and healing, as we gaze on you.

<><><><><><><><><><><><><><><><><><><><><><><><>

DANGER IN WITHDRAWING

At that time Jesus came from Galilee to the Jordan River so that John would baptize him.

—Matthew 3:13

Many theologians agree that we are wounded in community *and* that we heal in community. We need to surround ourselves with people who tell us that we don't have to perform to be loved. We are loved simply because we were born. We need physical reminders like smiles, handshakes, and hugs to remember who we are as beloved children of God. We need to say to one another and to hear that we are appreciated, that we are not alone, and that we are praying for one another.

Most importantly, we must recognize that we have a choice to be in relationship or to withdraw, just as Jesus had a choice in Matthew 3:13-17. Before his public ministry began, he could have chosen to remain anonymous or to run from his call (like Jonah). Instead, Jesus chose to come out and be baptized.

We, too, can choose to show up, take a risk, and be active in a group of believers. Or we can choose to remain isolated, cut off from God and others. We can choose to succumb to feelings of unworthiness and fear, disconnected from our own essential nature as dearly loved children of God. We can always choose sadness over joy, death over life, and fear over love. But God invites us to choose love and to claim our belovedness.

We can walk out of our hiding places, down into the river with Jesus, and be open to a new way of being in the world—being beloved. This is a kind of love that is so unfamiliar to us, requiring nothing, offering everything, never running out or wearing down, and available to all people all times in all places. Psalm 139 says, "LORD, you have examined me. You know me." God knows what we really want and is waiting with open arms to welcome us back to our own lives, ourselves, God's love, and our relationships with others.

When we choose to withdraw, Lord, remind us that community offers power and life. We are created to be together. Help us lean into one another, even when it is hard.

SELF-DEFEATING BEHAVIORS

*Remain in me, and I will remain in you. A branch can't produce
fruit by itself, but must remain in the vine. Likewise, you can't
produce fruit unless you remain in me.*

—John 15:4

Nothing prepared me for how my assault would change my perception of reality and myself. Afterward, I thought I was making my own choices when I decided to drink too much or have relationships with people I never would have dated before. I became someone I would not have previously respected. The change was slow, like dropping a live frog into lukewarm water before turning the heat up to boil. So I assumed it was normal or natural, perhaps even evolved.

In hindsight, my actions were none of those. My choices were self-defeating, chaining me to my identity as a victim. I leaned into a family legacy of addiction, dancing along the edge of "normal," but dangerously close to losing myself entirely. At the time, I didn't care. I felt something again, even if it was fear, anger, or disgust. I felt something after a long time of repressing my pain and truth. But one morning, after a particularly awful night, I looked into the mirror and said out loud, "Who are you anyway?"

Suddenly my mother's voice sprang into my mind. Before we left the house for dates in high school, she would always say, "Remember who you are!"

I realized that God could use my broken heart, shattered dreams, and terrible choices to draw me back into the fold of God's love and identity. I returned to God and slowly began to feel healthy again for the first time in ages. In time, I became someone again who I could love and respect.

◇◇◇◇◇◇◇◇◇◇◇◇◇◇◇◇◇◇◇◇◇◇◇◇◇◇◇◇◇◇◇◇◇◇◇◇

*Surprising God, we give you our lives full of chaos and brokenness.
As we wait for your healing touch, keep us rooted in your presence
and remind us of who we are. Speak, and give us the stillness to
hear your powerful words of renewal.*

◇◇◇◇◇◇◇◇◇◇◇◇◇◇◇◇◇◇◇◇◇◇◇◇◇◇◇◇◇◇◇◇◇◇◇◇

WILL I EVER FEEL NORMAL?

Stop worrying about tomorrow, because tomorrow will worry about itself. Each day has enough trouble of its own.

—Matthew 6:34

As a survivor of mental, physical, and sexual abuse, I attributed my strong gut feelings to an innate, even distinctly female, phenomenon. I never considered that my intuition could be an inheritance from my violent past until graduate school, where I read an article that pointed out that anticipating other people's action is necessary to survival in an abusive situation.

At some points in my life, my intuition and ability to anticipate the actions of others were helpful. But there were also times when I slipped into codependency or became a chameleon. Shifting my own desires and feelings to protect or nurture someone else seemed natural—what I should do if I loved someone or wanted to remain safe. It was so difficult to trust again and to stand on my own two feet, articulating and insisting on what I want and need to be healthy and happy.

God created us to be with one another, and when the time is right, we will likely risk some form of intimate relationship again. Perhaps it will be a friendship, a dating relationship, or even more—but until then, we need to focus on being truthful with ourselves. Keep asking yourself the tough questions. Keep insisting on a deeper level of honesty from yourself and others. What you have experienced has changed you, but in time you may learn that some scars bring along unexpected gifts and legacies.

<><><><><><><><><><><><><><><><><><><><><>

Receive my worry, Lord, with your creative sense of wholeness and goodness. Help me to accept this trauma, as you eventually shift my heart to risk trusting someone else again.

<><><><><><><><><><><><><><><><><><><><><>

RESTLESS REALIZATIONS

I will lie down and fall asleep in peace
because you alone, LORD, let me live in safety.

—Psalm 4:8

Sometimes starlight and shadows bring us closer to God. When we cannot see what lies around us, we could become more aware of what lies within us. After my assault and at various stages of recovery, I experienced insomnia. It felt like a curse at first, but over time I made peace with and even discovered some beauty in the darkest, sleepless nights.

Paul and Silas prayed down prison walls in the middle of the night (Acts 16). When the world is sleeping, God works overtime. Or maybe that's just that when we slow down enough, are still enough, stop wrestling with our feelings, and stop working so hard to avoid our pain, depression, anger, fear, self-loathing, loneliness, sadness, or [insert your struggle here]. Maybe then, in the silence, we can finally hear God speak to us.

If so, a sleepless night becomes an invitation to meet with God and to experience the blessing of love and acceptance. When we close our mouths and open our ears and hearts, we can begin to see ourselves as God sees us: worthy to be loved and cared for, precious children, created in the image of pure, undeserving, ecstatic, life-changing, unrestrained, revolutionary, awe-inspiring love.

When we allow God to fill us with this love, with this peace that passes understanding, we begin to see ourselves and others in a different way. Our patience grows, fears and doubts quiet, and we understand more and become capable of loving more. We begin to feel more connected to God and to one another. When our resentment melts, anger calms, and hatred dissolves, our hearts begin to heal.

Creator of the light and darkness, as we join you in the stillness of
restless nights, remind us that you are holy and wholly good. Help
us claim our birthright: to love you and ourselves, to be healed, and
to share your love with others.

LISTENING FOR GOD

While he was still speaking, look, a bright cloud overshadowed
them. A voice from the cloud said, "This is my Son whom I dearly
love. I am very pleased with him. Listen to him!" Hearing this, the
disciples fell on their faces, filled with awe.

—Matthew 17:5-6

In the 2010 film *Eat Pray Love*, actress Julia Roberts attempts to pray
for the first time while lying on her bathroom floor in the middle of
the night. She tentatively asks God what she should do about her
marriage. Finally, in near desperation, she cries out and then waits si-
lently. Soon, a quiet version of her own voice tells her to go back to bed.
Maybe God speaks like that—not a loud voice outside of us, but a small,
strong and sturdy little voice within us.

In this passage from Matthew, I imagine God's booming voice forc-
ing men to their knees in fear. But the text says *before* a voice was heard,
a bright cloud overshadowed them. What if this was enough to force the
disciples' gazes upwards in speechless wonder? What if, out of this small,
silent moment, each man heard a whisper in his own heart, perhaps even
in his own voice?

In the presence of pure holiness, of the all-mighty, all-powerful
God, it is normal to be quaking in your boots. Not that God wants to
scare or threaten us, but when we fully understand, even for just a moment, how deep and wide and high and great is the power of God's love
for us, then we must be overwhelmed with awe and sometimes even
afraid. We don't understand love like that; we have nothing to relate it to
or to help us grasp it. So we fall to our knees in silence, wait, and listen.

Come, Lord Jesus, and speak to us in still, strong, powerful ways
so that we may once again feel your presence and accept your
overflowing love for us.

PRAYER IN ACTION

Pray continually.

—1 Thessalonians 5:17

How is it possible to pray continually, especially while we wrestle with trauma and healing? When we experience violation, it can be difficult (or nearly impossible) to turn to God in prayer. I didn't want to address the painful fact that God had not prevented my assault or rescued me.

After some time, though, I began to miss my prayer life and gave it an awkward try. At first, I cried and screamed and even questioned whether God really existed. I was honest about my pain, doubt, and loneliness. A therapist had once told me that God had "big girl panties" and could handle the rawness of my emotions. She also said that God longs for our honesty because healing begins with our deepest truth. So I tried it, even though it wasn't easy or smooth.

Authentic prayer can take many forms, though. San Antonio chef Joan Cheever used her food truck to feed people who were hungry and homeless. In doing so, she broke a city ordinance and received a citation. Defending herself, she claimed that she had a right to practice her religion. The police officers told her to go to church and pray. She responded, "This is how I pray. I pray when I cook. I pray when I serve."

Sometimes, especially in the aftermath of disaster, we have trouble sitting still or folding our hands in prayer. Perhaps, though, we can wash laundry or dishes, pick up trash on the side of the road, or spend time with someone who is sick or grieving. These are all forms of prayer and can be ways to connect with God's transforming love.

◇◇◇◇◇◇◇◇◇◇◇◇◇◇◇◇◇◇◇◇◇◇◇◇◇◇◇◇◇◇◇◇

Move in me, Lord God, and show me ways that I can pray, both in word and in action, so that your healing can transform my anger, sadness, and pain.

◇◇◇◇◇◇◇◇◇◇◇◇◇◇◇◇◇◇◇◇◇◇◇◇◇◇◇◇◇◇◇◇

WHEN WORDS ARE NOT POSSIBLE

God is our refuge!

—*Psalm 62:8*

Years before I could talk about my sexual assault with anyone—when I could barely journal about my experiences without sobbing all over the page—I began to attend a weekly women's Bible study. I was a stranger and much younger than the others; I felt slightly distant from the group.

Our study focused on the stories of women throughout the Old and New Testaments. Even though I had read the Bible before, I had somehow overlooked these women, many of whom who had been violated and disregarded. My heart began to soften toward myself and toward the other women in the group.

One day, we discussed the gang rape and murder of a Levite's wife in Judges 19. (It is a brutal story; I do not recommend it when you are in the throes of trauma recovery.) We tackled the awful story and mourned for the woman who breathed her last on the threshold of a door that could have opened to protect her but did not. One woman lifted prayers for all who had been violated, harmed, and destroyed by violence, sexual or otherwise. We prayed for those who are currently teetering in thresholds, unsafe and alone. I sobbed quietly and said nothing, but these women understood.

There is a sisterhood, a brotherhood, a kinship for those who have survived great violence, shame, and suffering. Words do not have to be spoken for hearts to hear and support one another. In silence, sobs, or knowing glances, we are reminded that we are not alone.

<><><><><><><><><><><><><><><><><><><><><><><>

Thank you, gracious God, for others who have experienced the trauma of sexual violence and the way we can be for one another a source of hope, a reminder of you within and among us, even when words are not possible.

<><><><><><><><><><><><><><><><><><><><><><><>

WALKING THROUGH GRIEF

Even when I walk through the darkest valley,
*   I fear no danger because you are with me.*
Your rod and your staff—
*   they protect me.*

—*Psalm 23:4*

Everyone is forced to walk through the valley of the shadow of death at some point in their lives. For some, it is during an act of physical violence or sexual assault. For others, it is in losing a loved one or facing a serious illness. No matter what causes the valley's shadows to come over us, the path is well-worn.

Grief is disorienting and cumulative; when we are grieving, we can't distinguish the pain of our various losses, past and present. I can be crying about something I read in a book, and suddenly I am crying about my assault. The grief-memory of my assault is a tight little rock inside my soul. Experiencing another form of grief can send that rock ripping through my body, mind, and memory.

As a pastor, I have studied the clinical stages of grief: denial, anger, bargaining, depression, and acceptance. They have never felt linear to me—more like a jumbled mess or tangled knot in my daughter's otherwise silky hair. If I drew the steps on the floor like an instructor teaching a new dance, we would all end up on our rear ends trying to follow.

But we keep going; we keep dancing our crazy dance. If we stop, the tidal wave of grief threatens to drown us. Of course, we all need a break every now and then, but eventually we have to keep moving, even if it's incrementally. When we press on, we become aware that we are not alone; God is surprisingly close.

Even when the air is thin and I can barely breathe, God, give me
the strength to keep moving through this pain and toward your
light. I need to feel you with me to carry on.

BABY-STEPPING

> *My brothers and sisters, think of the various tests you encounter as occasions for joy. After all, you know that the testing of your faith produces endurance. Let this endurance complete its work so that you may be fully mature, complete, and lacking in nothing.*
>
> —James 1:2-4

How do we escape the darkness, fear, and pain and move toward God's light, peace, and love? When our minds and bodies are racked with such terrible memories or feelings, how can we ever move forward?

The best we can do is to face tough times with as much strength and hope as we can and invite God to carry us through. When I have endured suffering, God has used that seed of pain, watered it with love and the moisture of my own tears, and birthed a beautiful tree of life and hope from it. Trauma splits us open—which gives God a chance to re-form us, to make us stronger, braver, and more authentic. With God's help, our trials and weaknesses result in patience, perseverance, peace, and joy.

I take comfort in knowing that our pain can be transformed within us, making us whole again, healthy and lacking nothing. This is who we were created to be, even if we have to baby-step our way along until we get there.

◇◇◇◇◇◇◇◇◇◇◇◇◇◇◇◇◇◇◇◇◇◇◇◇◇◇◇◇◇◇

> *Go-between Sprit, remind us that we are not of this world, but of the kingdom of God. Renew our spirits and carry us when we cannot go on. Give us strength and courage, and let us shine the light of your love on all those around us.*

◇◇◇◇◇◇◇◇◇◇◇◇◇◇◇◇◇◇◇◇◇◇◇◇◇◇◇◇◇◇

HEALING ARTWORK

God created... [and] saw how good it was.

—*Genesis 1:21*

That same weekly women's Bible study just couldn't leave well enough alone! After we studied great mothers of faith, we decided to create a sort of tapestry, weaving together images of our own stories and those of our favorite Biblical women. I felt inadequate; art was not my strong suit.

To begin, our pastor invited us to draw how we were feeling. If we couldn't draw how we felt, we were to pick a favorite Bible story and draw it. Laughing nervously, I decided to work with the creation story from Genesis 1.

I thought about the power, creativity, and skill it took for God to create everything from nothing. Slowly, I drew a small red heart to signify God's love, the impetus for creation. Then I drew black swirls around it to indicate the darkness "in the beginning." I added yellow streaks for light, green lines for land, blue squiggles for water, and red marks to show God's ever-present love. Finally, I added little flowers and leaves. When I looked at my childish drawing, I saw chaos, the magnificent miracle of creation—but also the chaos in my own heart and life and in the lives of my Bible study friends.

Without meaning to, I *had* drawn how I was feeling: a jumbled mess, riddled with God's love and alive with the powerful possibilities of creation. The art wasn't aesthetically pleasing, but it was beautiful in its truth and became the basis for our tapestry. A tree of life grew out of the chaos and love—and I began to believe new life could also sprout from me.

Even in my darkness, Lord, you remind me that you are the source of all beginnings and creation. Shape my chaos into something beautiful and help me find ways to express myself through creative expression.

FINDING STILLNESS

Be still, and know that I am God!
—Psalm 46:10 (NRSV)

At one phase of recovery, I was struck with searing momentary flashbacks. Such trauma reactions can be triggered by feelings, sensations, or triggering words, but the flashbacks would strike in completely unrelated moments, too. I'd be walking down a sidewalk and suddenly I'd be slamming into a glass table. Almost immediately, the image disappeared, but I could barely remain standing. Or I'd be having coffee with a friend, talking about her life, and I would feel a hand tighten around my throat and squeeze. I would cough and sputter and look at her as if I didn't know her. It was scary for me and for my loved ones.

I wrestled with my flashbacks. At times I excused myself and went to the bathroom to cry and shake. Other times, if I felt safe enough, I explained my reaction, sometimes using a few tentative words and sometimes pouring out my whole story. What proved most hepful for me was, when possible, to sit or lie down, be still, and breathe deeply.

Being still has never come naturally to me. Now I am learning to be still and listen for God's voice. I may not appear calm on the outside, but I am learning that a still heart is balm to my wounded soul. Stillness connects me to God, and, even if it looks like I'm not doing anything at all, I know I am doing the hard work of healing when I rest and breathe.

Wrap your loving arms around me, God, especially during the terrible flashbacks and jarring memories. Remind me that there is peace beyond tragedy, resurrection after death, and your healing presence in the stillness.

COMFORT IN PRAYER

With a strong hand and outstretched arm—
God's faithful love lasts forever!

—*Psalm 136:12*

There are many times that I am unsure what to do. Should I speak out or be silent? Choose this path or that one? What is the most loving action I can take right now?

For me, open and honest prayer best helps me figure out what to do when. But praying nice, like "playing nice," doesn't get us very far. Healing from trauma is not a nice, neat, or easy process. It is hard work, painful and messy; there are no one-size-fits-all directions.

Don't be afraid to pray, even if you think you are doing it wrong, even if you are angry or broken, if you blame God, or doubt God's existence. Bring your deepest questions and biggest feelings to God. Maybe you wonder where God was during your assault or why God doesn't strike down the person who hurt you.

Getting to the bottom of our trauma takes tapping into those deepest, most awful thoughts and feelings. From that lowest, worst possible point, we can slowly look up. In those vulnerable moments we can see God most clearly. Perhaps God is reaching out to us like a loving parent, grandparent, or friend, inviting us to curl up in God's lap for a while and rest. When we feel deep loss and loneliness, we can also feel that lap underneath us, those outstretched arms around us, and those strong hands comforting us.

The Creator of heaven and earth can handle our strongest emotions and darkest fears, but only if we bring them to God.

Wrap us in your love, Holy One, so that we may sense and know
that your love is without boundaries or limits. Give us courage to
pray even in doubt and darkness.

RESTORATIVE COMMUNITY

I've clearly seen my people oppressed.... I've heard their cry of injustice.... I know about their pain. I've come down to rescue them... in order to take them out of that land and bring them to... a land that's full of milk and honey.

—*Exodus 3:7-8*

The ancient Hebrew people had been enslaved in Egypt for many years when God spoke these words of hope. Though their experience was terrible and terribly unjust, God did not let it define them; God had more in store for them. God redeemed them; God empowered and encouraged them to break free, to leave their life of suffering and slavery behind, and to seek a new beginning filled with goodness.

What was true for ancient Israel is true for us today: God wants to rescue us from the pain and injustice and give us a new beginning. What happened to us does not define us! We may bear the scars and memories of violence, but God can help us break free of the chains of fear, guilt, and shame as we heal.

As humans, we are created in and for community, and healing is most effective as part of a community. The Hebrew people weren't restored as individuals; they were restored as a people. When we open ourselves up to others and allow them to do the same, we heal each other. Reaching out and being part of any group can be scary, but the benefits far outweigh the risks.

◇◇◇◇◇◇◇◇◇◇◇◇◇◇◇◇◇◇◇◇◇◇◇◇◇◇◇◇◇◇◇◇◇◇◇◇

Lead me to a place where I can help and be helped, heal and be healed. Help me release my identity as a victim and live into my identity as a survivor and a co-creator of healing alongside you.

◇◇◇◇◇◇◇◇◇◇◇◇◇◇◇◇◇◇◇◇◇◇◇◇◇◇◇◇◇◇◇◇◇◇◇◇

REBELLION OF LOVE

Jesus came near and spoke to them, "I've received all authority in heaven and on earth."

—Matthew 28:18

Growing up, I thought rules were made to be challenged or broken. I wanted to bust my own path through life, like a hiker in dense woods with a machete, slicing through anything or anybody in my way. In the end, I realized that this approach didn't really solve my problems and even hurt me.

As survivors of assault and trauma, we tend to have a complicated relationship with authority. It's important for us to claim our own power after we have been rendered so powerless. But constantly challenging authority—whether it's the authority of certain people, like our boss or our parents, or entities we had previously given authority to, such as God or our own personal moral code—usually doesn't serve us well in the long run.

Jesus also had a complicated relationship with the authorities of his time. He targeted his acts of rebellion wisely instead of constantly asserting his power over the people around him. In doing so, he concentrated his personal power in order to effect the greatest possible change. We still live into his legacy thousands of years later.

We don't have to obey every authority all the time, but neither do we have to continually disregard it. In time, we learn when to rebel and when to obey, when to submit and when to fight back. We channel our personal power, choose our battles carefully, and make our decisions wisely. We learn to *act* rather than *react*.

Give me a wise and discerning heart, God, so that I know when to lead, when to fight, and when to follow. Shape my independent heart into a healthy dependence on you.

TRUTH-TELLING

A certain man was there who had been sick for thirty-eight years.... Jesus said to him, "Get up! Pick up your mat and walk."
—John 5:5, 8

Words are powerful. I can easily say that I was "sexually assaulted," but at times, I choke on the word "rape." I do not want to be a woman who was raped. I do not want the ugliness and the shame of that word to wash over me.

My sexual assault was not my first experience of violence—or my last. As a teenager, I took the brunt of my alcoholic father's rage. I logically understood that none of it was my fault, but I secretly feared that he was right—so I told no one. That changed the night the police called. I drove my mother to the hospital, and behind that flimsy curtain, I told her about everything: the threats, the accusations, and the violence. I could see her heart breaking. It was awful. But telling the truth was the first crack that let the light in, and after that, things slowly began to change and to get better.

When Jesus heals the man who had been sick for 38 years, he does it with his words alone. The man speaks his truth that he wants to be healed, and Jesus responds with words of restoration. Like Jesus', our words can bring healing, restore strength and faith, offer hope, and provide support for others around us. Words of truth can even bring new life to our own souls.

Is there a truth that you are hiding, possibly even from yourself? Could you imagine what light and healing might be let in if you share your truth?

∞∞∞∞∞∞∞∞∞∞∞∞∞∞∞∞∞∞∞∞∞∞∞∞∞∞∞∞∞∞∞

Give me the courage to speak my truth out loud, Lord, even when I am scared, even when someone else refuses to hear it. Begin the mighty work of healing in me!

∞∞∞∞∞∞∞∞∞∞∞∞∞∞∞∞∞∞∞∞∞∞∞∞∞∞∞∞∞∞∞

SPEAKING OUT

*God **said**, "Let there be light." And so light appeared.*
—Genesis 1:3 (emphasis added)

The year after I was assaulted, I worked on a rape crisis hotline. At first, I was afraid that the work would trigger my trauma and throw me spiraling back into chaos, but it had the exact opposite effect. Being able to speak to men and women who had been through, in some way, something that I had been through, made me feel strong and useful. Being raped had broken me down and left me feeling powerless, scared and weak. Talking about it helped me conquer my demons of fear and shame.

Sharing my story and encouraging others to share theirs gave me strength and hope. Yes, it was (and still can be) difficult to hear so many overwhelming stories of violence and abuse. But through the tears and pain, I could hear something happen. Both in myself and in those on the other end of the line, something began to shift and grow; we began to envision, and then speak out loud, our wishes that the future could be different. Just as God spoke the universe into being, we sometimes speak our own healing into reality.

Of course, not everyone can share their stories out loud or with another person. We must be gentle and honest with ourselves, waiting for the right time. Finding a safe space, possibly with a friend, therapist, fellow survivor, or even a journal or blog, can open the doors to a restorative relationship and help you find your voice.

Help me to speak, God, in whatever ways I can, and even if my words are never shared or uttered out loud, create through them something new and beautiful in me.

GRATITUDE

As a result of having strong roots in love, I ask that you'll have the power to grasp love's width and length, height and depth, together with all believers. I ask that you'll know the love of Christ.
—Ephesians 3:17-19

During a difficult season of my life, a friend challenged me to keep a gratitude journal. Every time I heard a church bell ring (which was frequent, given that I was living in Europe at the time), I was to stop, take out my pocket journal, and write down something that made me happy, and give thanks.

Perhaps doing something similar could be helpful to you. I found it helpful to have a prompt, about every hour, so that I was forced to identify something that made me happy even if I wasn't feeling like it. It turned out that even when I could not feel it, God was with me. Perhaps you could set an alarm or notification on your phone to encourage you to write, or connect it to some common occurrence, like receiving a text message or hearing music. If you feel out of God's reach, it is possible that saying thank you will help you reconnect.

I still journal, recording what is going well in my heart and life. Some days the gratitude overflows and fills up page after page. Other days, I stare at a blank page, struggling to see anything good. The practice, though, helps me notice my blessings. I also notice changes in the way I perceive myself and others, and in how I deal with problems. Even when I'm struggling, I feel emotionally happier and physically healthier when I journal.

Reconnecting to God through gratitude reminds me of my "roots," God's love that holds me steady.

Pour your love into my heart and life, Lord. Remind me of your gifts and surprising blessings, and help me return to my rootedness in your love.

LOVING MYSELF

He responded, "You must love the Lord your God with all your heart, with all your being, with all your strength, and with all your mind, and love your neighbor as yourself."

—*Luke 10:27*

I don't have much trouble loving God and other people. But loving myself can be hard. It is safer and easier to love something abstract than to love the person I see in the mirror every day, with all her embarrassing jiggly bits, emotional scars, and other perceived imperfections.

Loving myself was a long and tough road, but it began by making peace with my past, my demons, my sins, shortfalls, and failings. It required a level of honesty with myself that was painful to witness and bear. I had become an expert at hiding my shadow side and pretending that everything was ok. But that was not self-love; it was theater, and it got me nowhere.

God knows our most intimate thoughts and feelings, even when the stage lights are off. God formed us in our mother's wombs before we were born (Jer 1:4-5) and God knew what we would become, down to this very day. We can't hide, and we shouldn't try. God's love is incomprehensible, so different from any other type of love we have ever felt or experienced. It doesn't have to be earned or purchased. It simply is. The more we are able to let ourselves experience and embrace God's love for us, the more we will be able to see ourselves through those same loving eyes.

Come, Holy Spirit, so that we might see ourselves rightly, no better or worse than anyone else, but completely accepted and beloved by you.

REEMBODIMENT

Israel, listen! Our God is the LORD! Only the LORD!
—Deuteronomy 6:4

Some time after my assault, a friend invited me to join her yoga class. As I laid on the mat for the very first time, I noticed how disassociated I had become from my own body. I could barely lie flat on the floor without pain somewhere. I felt like I was failing at yoga—which made me feel like a failure in life. I remembered all the ways I had failed myself and others over the years.

While I basked in shame and hopelessness, the instructor asked us to let our thoughts slip away. We were to focus on our breathing, counting gently as we breathed in and out, trying to extend the breath in both directions. Slowly, I began to narrow my focus onto my breath. The Hebrew name of God, *Yah-weh*, is formed as we breathe. We open ourselves to God as breathe in the openness of the *yah* and release our stress, fear, and pain as we exhale the *weh*. Each breath can be an invitation to the Holy One who gives us, again and again, the gift of our next breath.

Breathing deeply brought me into an awareness of God's presence and back into my own body. It helped me to notice my physical pain and the ways I had ignored my needs or failed to care for myself. Rather than focusing on my failures, I was now weeping with joy that I could be in my body again, connected to myself (including my pain) and breathing in tandem with a group of imperfect but beautiful children of God.

Thank you, persistent God, for using every moment in our lives to get our attention and remind us that you are with us. Help us to see and to welcome you with each breath we take.

HEALING TOUCH

Moved with pity, Jesus stretched out his hand and touched him.
—Mark 1:41 (NRSV)

After my assault, I went for many years without getting a massage, which I had previously enjoyed a great deal. The thought of someone touching me again was unbearable. I worried that I might not ever be able to enjoy another massage or a normal intimate relationship of any kind. I worried that a violent touch had broken me for good.

In the scripture above, Jesus was willing to touch a man with a terrible skin disease even though the contact would make Jesus ritually unclean. He healed the man's physical problem and returned the man to his social community. In so many words, and with a powerful touch, Jesus said, "Welcome back from your isolation, your darkness and your pain. Welcome back the world of loving touch and community." Touch can be healing.

It is natural to want to deflect physical touch after an assault. Still, being touched in gentleness, kindness, and love reminds our physical bodies and our souls that we deserve these good gifts. Though your body and spirit have been violated, you deserve the comfort of physical touch.

Fill us with compassion for ourselves, Lord, and let us seek out the power of healing touch in whatever form we can accept, as an offering of love from you yourself.

FORGIVING

*I know the plans I have in mind for you, declares the LORD; they
are plans for peace . . . to give you a future filled with hope.*

—*Jeremiah 29:11*

t took me seven long years to forgive him. I am not pushing you to
forgive if you are not ready. You may never be ready, and that's okay.
It's not something we can set a timeline for. It is not your responsibility to forgive your perpetrator. But many people do find forgiveness
healing and empowering.

When I was ready to consider forgiveness, I was simple but brutally
honest in my prayers: "I don't want to forgive, God. I am angry and
hurt, not ready to let go. If you want forgiveness, please do it through
me. I don't have the strength or desire. If you want forgiveness, then
work a miracle in me. Melt my anger, wash away my tears, soften the
terrible memories, and help me to see him as you see him, a beloved
child of God. I can't, I don't want to . . . but if it's your plan for me, I'll
give you the space to do it in me."

That's it. There are millions of books written about forgiveness, but
for me, it was as simple and as heartbreakingly complex, as that. I would
never forget the painful memories, but as time passed, they didn't burn
and cut me anymore. They became like a scar that is visible but not
bothersome.

Forgiveness happened in God's timing without any push from me.
It was like building up a muscle, though, and later I found it easier to
forgive others who hurt me.

*When your time is right, gentle God, soften my heart toward the
person/people who hurt me most, even if that is myself. Do not let
my anger and pain drown out your love!*

CHOOSING HEALTHY
RELATIONSHIPS

Dear friends, let's love each other, because love is from God, and everyone who loves is born from God and knows God. The person who doesn't love does not know God, because God is love.

—1 John 4:7-8

I married years after my assault. My husband was kind at first but took a terrible turn over time. Struggling with anxiety and depression, he began to drink too much. He eventually became cruel and violent. I was repeating the pattern of violence from my childhood.

I still fault myself for not recognizing the pattern earlier. The process was slower the second time around, so I missed the signs...or chose to ignore them. On the heels of an alcoholic father and a sexual assault, the last thing I wanted to do was admit that my marriage included violence. But there it was. This trauma reared its ugly head, again and again, until I broke the cycle and cried out: "No More!"

Years later, I married again, and now have a wonderfully kind husband and two bright and tender-hearted children. My journey to identify and break my patterns of violence took years of gut-wrenching therapy and spiritual direction. I needed patience and tenacity to learn what it was like to be in a healthy, non-codependent relationship. But the hard work was worth it.

Some people ask how they could ever trust someone in an intimate relationship again. I say, establish trust and safety. Build a relationship based on mutuality and understanding. Know your boundaries. And, when you are ready, just be brave and give it a try.

◇◇

Give us wisdom to know when to pull back and when to plunge ahead, God. Fill us with your love and help us to find safe, healing ways to share love with others.

◇◇

GUARD YOUR HEART

If you lie down, you won't be terrified.
When you lie down, your sleep will be pleasant.

—Proverbs 3:24

Sometimes I pretend my assault hasn't changed me. I like to think that healing means I am just the same as I was before the attack. But I'm not. Things that didn't bother me before affect me now in ways I can't deny. For example, television shows and movies about rape rob me of sweet sleep and give me vivid nightmares, even years after my assault. They hit too close to home, so I choose not to watch them. I don't want to open myself up to that sort of re-traumatization.

As you heal, you may notice reactions that surprise you. We can't avoid everything that triggers our trauma responses, but sometimes we do have the choice of whether to make ourselves vulnerable in that particular way. We can guard our hearts.

You are the expert on you, the one who knows best what you need to find peace. You also sense what is unhealthy for you. You are in charge of your choices. Healing is a very individual process, and it takes time. Pay attention to the advice of professionals and people who love, but also listen to your own body, mind, heart, and soul. God will whisper what you need, and you can choose how to respond.

I can't change my circumstances, Lord, but I can take steps to protect myself from further harm. Break down my bitterness. Assure me that I can safely trust you again.

TRAUMA MUSCLES

*Therefore, I'm all right with weaknesses, insults, disasters,
harassments, and stressful situations for the sake of Christ, because
when I'm weak, then I'm strong.*

—*2 Corinthians 12:10*

Many years after my assault, I experienced another form of trauma. My family lived in a small town rocked by a natural disaster. We were loving our cute apartment on a river, my first job as a pastor, and our newborn baby girl. But then public sirens went off in the dead of night, and I received a phone call that my little church would be the first shelter for those who had been flooded out of their homes.

Floods, like fires, tornadoes, hurricanes, and other forms of natural disaster, are not natural at all. They are frightening, life-threatening, super-voltage shocks to our limbic system (that little part of our brains that kicks us into fight, flight, or freeze mode when it senses threats). Like grief, this biological response is stored in our physical, emotional, and psychological bodies—and when it is unleashed, it is difficult for us to differentiate between various forms of threat and trauma, past or present.

As I worked through the night and day (and then through the next weeks, months and years), I comforted those who had lost their homes, pets, and loved ones. My limbic system was working overtime, but I didn't experience fear or the desire to run. I had survived trauma much worse than this. In doing so, I had strengthened my limbic "muscles" and could draw from those reserves to help others cope. I had discovered the depths of my strength and shared from there. Surviving and overcoming trauma uniquely prepares us to help others in need.

<><><><><><><><><><><><><><><><><><><><><><><><><>

*Reveal to us the depth of our own strength in you, Lord Jesus, and
show us how we might use what we have suffered and survived to
help others cope and thrive.*

<><><><><><><><><><><><><><><><><><><><><><><><><>

CHOSEN

The LORD your God chose you to be his own treasured people beyond all others… because the LORD loved you.

—Deuteronomy 7:6b, 8a

It is rare for me to look in the mirror and feel deeply chosen—to believe that of all the people on this planet, God has chosen ME as a special treasure and loves ME uniquely and completely. God loves me, not in spite of my faults and flaws, but because of them. My weaknesses, shortcomings, and not-quite-there-yet traits offer fertile ground for God's work of healing, love, acceptance and empowerment. Being honest about my pain and vulnerabilities opens me up to receive God's love and inspires authenticity in others. I'll show you my pain if you show me yours.

One of the greatest mysteries of my life and my faith is the logic of God's unconditional, unchanging, no-questions-asked, no-deposit-required, no-input-from-me-needed, nothing-can-separate-us-from-its-source *love*. How can I accept and understand a love that is unlike any other kind of love I have ever experienced? A love that is given so generously and extravagantly?

Maybe you are like me and prefer to work to earn your keep. If I work hard for something, then I am entitled to it. If I have earned something, I can claim it, control it, own it, and hold onto it. But I cannot and do not need to manipulate God's love. As hard as it can be to believe, God's love isn't going away. It will always be with me.

Continue to lead us on a healing journey, gracious God, and give us the courage to see ourselves as you see us: beloved, chosen, and whole.

NOTES

INTRODUCTION

1. The story of "Mary" is indeed inspired by one of my first therapy clients. Her name, of course, has been changed, and the details provided about her are not unique to her story; rather, they are taken from my experiences over the course of my career working with many adult survivors of childhood sexual abuse.

2. "Statistics About Sexual Violence Fact Sheet," National Sexual Violence Resource Center, 2015, http://www.nsvrc.org/sites/default/files/2015-01/publications _nsvrc_factsheet_media-packet_statistics-about-sexual-violence_0.pdf.

1. PSYCHOLOGICAL AND PHYSIOLOGICAL EFFECTS OF SEXUAL ASSAULT

1. Bessel van der Kolk, "VIDEO: When Is It Trauma? Bessel van der Kolk Explains," *Psychotherapy Networker Blog*, January 11, 2017, https://www.psychother apynetworker.org/blog/details/311/video-when-is-it-trauma-bessel-van-der-kolk -explains.

2. "Facts about Women and Trauma," American Psychological Association, 2018, http://www.apa.org/advocacy/interpersonal-violence/women-trauma.aspx.

3. American Psychiatric Association, *Diagnostic and Statistical Manual of Mental Disorders, Fifth Edition* (Arlington, VA: American Psychiatric Association, 2013), 271–72.

4. Bessel van der Kolk, *The Body Keeps the Score: Brain, Mind and Body in the Healing of Trauma* (New York: Penguin Books, 2014), 98–99.

5. V. J. Felitti, R. F. Anda, D. Nordenberg, D. F. Williamson, A. M. Spitz, V. Edwards, M. P. Koss, and J. S. Marks, "Relationship of Childhood Abuse and Household Dysfunction to Many of the Leading Causes of Death in Adults," *American Journal of Preventive Medicine* 14, no. 4 (1998): 245–58, http://doi.org/10.106150749 -3797(98)00017-8.

6. "Adverse Childhood Experiences (ACEs)," Centers for Disease Control and Prevention, 2018, https://www.cdc.gov/violenceprevention/acestudy/index.html.

7. Van der Kolk, *The Body Keeps the Score*, 4.

2. RECLAIMING YOUR POWER

1. Susan Brownmiller, *Against Our Will: Men, Women, and Rape* (New York: Simon and Schuster, 1975).

2. G. Kalra and D. Bhugra, "Sexual violence against women: Understanding cross-cultural intersections," *Indian Journal of Psychiatry* 55, no. 3 (2013): 244–49, http://doi.org/10.4103/0019-5545.117139.

3. B. A. McPhail, "Feminist Framework Plus: Knitting feminist theories of rape etiology into a comprehensive model," *Trauma, Violence & Abuse* 17, no. 3 (2015): 314–29, http://doi.org/10.1177/1524838015584367.

4. "The Criminal Justice System: Statistics," Rape, Abuse and Incest National Network, 2015, https://www.rainn.org/statistics/criminal-justice-system.

3. DISARMING SHAME

1. Brené Brown, *The Gifts of Imperfection* (Center City, MN: Hazelton, 2010), 39.

2. C. Feiring and L. Tasks, "The persistence of shame following sexual abuse: A longitudinal look at risk and recovery," *Child Maltreatment* 10, no. 4 (2005): 337–49. Also, C. Negrao, G. Bonanno, J. Noll, F. Putnam, and P. Trickett, "Shame, Humiliation and Childhood Sexual Abuse: Distinct Contributions and Emotional Coherence" *Child Maltreatment* 10, no. 4 (2005): 350–63.

3. "Reporting of Sexual Violence Incidents," National Institute of Justice, 2010, https://www.nij.gov/topics/crime/rape-sexual-violence/Pages/rape-notification.aspx.

4. Brown, *The Gifts of Imperfection*, 40.

4. PRACTICING SELF-COMPASSION

1. Kristin Neff, *Self-compassion: The Proven Power of Being Kind to Yourself* (New York: William Morrow, a Division of Harper Collins, 2015).

2. E. L. Worthington, C. V. Witvliet, P. Pietrini, and A. J. Miller, "Forgiveness, health and well-being: a review of evidence for emotional and decisional forgiveness, dispositional forgivingness, and reduced unforgiveness," *Journal of Behavioral Medicine* 30, no. 4 (2007): 291–302.

3. Ibid.

5. RESOURCES FOR CONTINUED HEALING

1. J. E. Taylor and S. T. Harvey, "Effects of psychotherapy with people who have been sexually assaulted: a meta-analysis," *Aggression and Violent Behavior* 14, no. 5 (2009): 273–85.

2. "Find Help Near You," Rape, Abuse and Incest National Network, 2018, https://centers.rainn.org.